Postmarked To Heaven

Sabrina Fernandez

BookLeaf Publishing

India | USA | UK

Dedication

This collection of poems is humbly dedicated to You,
Dear Jesus.

Your love, grace, and redemption inspired every word,
every line, and every heartbeat within these pages.

May this book glorify Your name, touch hearts,
and guide souls closer to Your eternal love.

Preface

Scrawled on tear-stained pages, mailed to the Only One who understands- Jesus!

'Postmarked to Heaven' is my raw correspondence with Jesus – 21 uncensored letters of brokenness, doubt, and redemption.

 Dive into this intimate exchange and discover the beauty of surrender. May these poems inspire you to embrace vulnerability with God and find solace in His presence.

Acknowledgements

They prayed for me before I took my first breath, and dragged me to church every Sunday thereafter – Mom, Dad, and Nana Penelope, your selfless devotion planted seeds of faith that blossomed into my soul.

Thank you for all the love and care, I'm so blessed to be on the receiving end of it. I love y'all so very much!🖤

1. Shadowed Doubts

In shadowed corners of my soul, doubts reside
Whispers of fear, a heart that's divided
I read the words, "You recruit from pits, not pedestals
high"
But faith falters, for I don't see it in my sky

Questions swirl like autumn leaves in wind
"Do You truly seek the broken, or just the kin?"
My heart cries out, "Jesus, show me Your design"
For in darkness, doubt's sharp teeth entwine

Still, I cling to echoes of Your gentle tone
A flicker of hope in this doubt-scarred zone
But will Your love be near, and make my heart feel at
home
And lead me out of darkness to a brighter throne?

2. Fault Lines Of Faith

My prayers fall like rain on barren ground
Seeds of hope wither, no response is found
I cry out to You, Jesus, but silence reigns
Like fault lines shifting, my faith sustains

I plead with empty hands, a heart on fire
But heavens seem brass, my words a tired desire
I'm praying through the tremors, of a soul on shaky ground
As fault lines of doubt fracture, my trust draws near

Tears fall like aftershocks, my soul exposed
I'm left to wonder, Jesus, do You hear my cries?
To feel my desperate pain, my heart's deep sighs?
Or am I praying to fault lines, in vain?
And will my fragile faith survive the strain?

3. Beyond The Bend

Beyond the heart is lost in wilderness, Jesus, I roam
Searching for Your footsteps, a guiding light to call home

Every path looks uncertain, like shadows on the wall
I'm longing for Your presence, beyond the bend of it all

In turbulent storms, I cry out for Your gentle hand
To still the raging waves, to calm this troubled land

My soul clings to Your promise, a lifeline in the night
Jesus, lead me through darkness, to Your loving light
Tears dry on my cheeks, as I whisper Your name

You meet me beyond the bend, where love and peace reign
And will you hold my heart together like pieces of a broken frame?

4. Anxiety's Ink Blot Stains

Anxiety's inkblots spread, Jesus, like stains on my soul
Obscuring Your presence, making faith's contours whole

Unclear thoughts bleed together, a Rorschach test of fear
I search for Your likeness, but darkness draws near

Inkblots of doubt suffocate, crushing heart's gentle flame
Leaving only shadows, where love and peace once
claimed

My mind's a shattered mirror, reflections distorted and
worn
Jesus, restore clarity, let Your light reborn

Tears fall like ink droplets, as I call out Your name
In prayer that your peace diffuses anxiety's darkest
inkblot stain

5. The In-Between Hush

5

In silence's hollow, Jesus, I search for Your voice
Uncertainty echoes, a haunting, empty choice
The in-between hush suffocates, where shadows play

I'm lost in life's pauses, grasping for a fading ray
Fear's dark thoughts deceive, obscuring heart's desire
To hear Your gentle words, my soul's deepest fire

In stillness, doubts assail, like thieves in endless night
Jesus, speak into silence, shine Your light on my plight
Will Your presence dispel darkness in this hollowed
space?

6. Midnight's Cartography

Midnight's cartography unfolds, a map of my soul's night
Twisted contours of fear, shading areas devoid of light
Rambling thoughts like uncharted seas, crashing on
despair's shore
Anxiety's dark longitude pulls me off-course

Depression's heavy fog obscures life's familiar terrain
I'm lost, Jesus, without a compass, in this inner world's
dark pain
Yet, in midnight's darkest hour, I search for Your guiding
star

A beacon to navigate heart's uncharted territories near
and far
Can Your love illuminate the darkness that I am?

In darkness, I'll hold to Your promise, a gentle, loving
hand
An anchor for my soul, in life's turbulent, uncertain land
Will You lead me through the shadows, to a brighter
promised land?

7. Uncovering Truth: But Will I Recognize It?

In doubt's buried city, I excavate my soul's deepest
ground
Searching for Your hidden treasures, Jesus, beneath
uncertainty's mound
Fear's rubble obscures the entrance, to trust's ancient,
hidden way
I'm digging through shadows, Jesus – uncover truth with
me each day

Doubt's dusty artifacts deceive, masking Your presence
from sight
I'm uncovering slowly, Jesus – reveal Your love in
morning light
Will Your gentle brush remove the dirt, exposing heart's
deepest truth tonight?

Like an archivist handling fragile scrolls, I ponder life's
design
Why do shadows fall on good hearts, and darkness touch
what's divine?
Bad things befall the innocent – a mystery that cuts like
a knife
Do You see our suffering, Jesus, or do our tears fall

without Your life?

When will You unravel this enigma, and bring clarity to
our pain?
How long must we wait for answers, Jesus – until love's
truth reigns?

8. Dawns Awakening

In dawn's soft light, I turn to You, Jesus
my heart once shrouded, now slowly breaks through
fears and doubts that long had held me cold
begin to thaw, as faith's warm light unfolds

With every breath, I whisper low
"You were here, Jesus, even in the darkest woe"
I'm starting to see, through tears and pain
You piecing the puzzle pieces again

In this calm dawn, my soul revives
as trust takes root, and heartaches subside
I'm learning to trust, Jesus, Your design
a masterpiece, where every piece aligns

Slowly clarity's soft light ascends
and I behold, Your love that never ends
in every moment, joy and strife
You were here, Jesus, working all things right

9. Unspooling The Narrative

Jesus, I hold the book of life, its pages unsealed
each day a new chapter, slowly revealed to me
You, Author of my life, write with gentle hand
at first, the story blurred, but now I understand Your
plan

Like a novel unfolding, plot twists come to light
characters of joy and pain take shape in the night
subplots of struggle weave into the main theme
and Your sovereign plan starts to be seen

As I read on, chapters merge into a coherent tale
my trust in You grows, Jesus, never to fail
I'm learning to trust the next chapter's unknown
for You, dear Author, write with love forever sown

With every new day, another chapter unfolds
I'm slowly trusting You, Jesus, Author of my soul
to script each new page, and make my story whole.

10. Beyond My Reflection

In Mirrors of self, I search for my name
but reflections fade into a distant flame
until I gaze into Your eyes, Jesus, and see
a beauty beyond mine

Your grace, a radiant light, shines deep within
exposing depths where fears and doubts locked me in
in shattered remnants, Your love pieces me anew
and I behold, in Your reflection, a heart renewed

In fragile frames of mine, Your strength takes hold
"Your grace is sufficient for me" – my heart is told
the echoes of inadequacy grow faint and cold
as Your sufficient love, Jesus, young and old, makes me
bold

With every glance into Your eyes, I see
a reflection of grace, wild and carefree
beyond my own, a beauty starts to shine
in Your majestic reflection, my true self aligns

11. Rooted In The Storm

When life's tornadoes twist, and balance snaps
like a tree in torrential rains, my roots collapse
but deep within, a spark remains
a ember of faith, glowing like a winter's flame

I keep my eyes anchored on Your horizon line
Jesus, my Lighthouse in the storm, guiding me through
life's turbulent brine
with You at my right hand, I'm moored like a ship in a
stormy sea
my heart regains balance, buoyed by faith's gravity

Like a taproot digging deep into the earth
I'll sink my trust in You, Jesus, my unshakeable birth
through trials' fiery furnace, my roots will grow strong
like a sequoia weathering wildfires, all day long

With every thunderclap that booms outside my door
I'll keep my gaze fixed on You, like a sailor riding out a
stormy roar
and stand firm on the Rock that never crumbles or shifts
my balance restored, my heart rooted in Your steadfast
cliffs

12. The Puzzle Pieces of Providence

In life's grand puzzle, pieces scattered lie
chaotic fragments of a larger picture's frame
yet deep within, a gentle murmur reassures my soul
"Trust My plan, child, every piece makes you whole"

I search for comfort in Your sovereign hand
where every detail, every thread is planned
no stray strand, no misplaced fragment remains
all woven into harmony with purpose, love, and gain

In challenges' dark pieces, I find a spark
a glow of purpose, igniting embark
on a journey where every step, every fall
fits into Your masterpiece, standing tall

And when I feel like just a single piece
adrift, alone, without a clear release
I remember I'm part of a grand design
unique, yet interconnected, a puzzle piece refined

With every fragment, You create a work of art
a masterpiece of love, beating in my heart
Romans 8:28 shines, a guiding, hopeful light

"And we know that in all things God works for the good of those who love him"

13. Moments In The Margin

In twilight's hush, where shadows softly fall
like velvet night's dark petals, unfolding all
a glimmer seeps, a fissure of pure light
kindling hidden paths, through endless night

In secret chambers of my soul's deep core
a promise stirs, a love letter penned on my heart's
darkest shore
inked on the parchment of my heart's innermost page
a mystery unfolds, like a rose in secret age

In overlooked hours, tucked between life's loud lines
like hidden frescoes in ancient, weathered shrines
I discover beauty in love's subtle, gentle might
a beacon piercing fear's dark veil, banishing endless
night

In silence between life's thunderous, crashing seas
I hear the still small voice, a gentle breeze that frees
the margins of my heart, where love's wildflower blooms
and breakthroughs unfold, like sunrise conquering
gloom

14. Pathways Illuminated, Heart Aglow

Jesus, as dawn's rose petals unfold, Your splendor shines
bathing pathways in amber light, like molten gold that
twines
around my soul's deep contours, a gentle, fiery stream
igniting inner lanterns, that illuminate my dream

With every step, a lotus flower of promise blooms in me
unfurling petals of hope, in life's uncertain perfumed
rooms, I see
Your heart remains a burning oasis, a desert flame
guiding me through shifting dunes, where love's mirage
becomes a claim

In pathways illuminated, I find my sacred grove with
You
a sanctuary of peace, where love's ancient wisdom roves
and whispers true
my heart aglow, a constellation of sparkling lights
reflecting the universe's beauty, on this inner, velvet
night

Through life's winding roads, Your glow will be my
constant light

illuminating hidden patterns, like constellations inside
pathways illuminated, heart aglow, I'll navigate and
reside
in the warm, golden essence of Your love, where my
spirit abides

15. Gratitude's Gentle Hum

Jesus, Your presence harmonizes my soul
a gentle hum resonates like a soft piano melody whole
warmth vibrates through my being like a cello's mellow
tone
as I breathe in the harmony of Your love – a sweet, sweet
song

Your grace is a master composer, orchestrating my life's
refrain
weaving together discordant notes into a beautiful,
soaring strain
like humming bees gathering nectar, my heart collects
Your grace
storing up sweetness, overflowing with praise

In Your abundance, I find a sense of rhythm – steady as a
drumbeat strong
my spirit sways like a dancer moving to the music all
day long
Your care is a gentle vibrato, soothing my soul's deepest
pain
quenching thirst like a refreshing melody that remains

My heart orchestrates a symphony of devotion
every note a soulful declaration, a love-infused emotion

19

16. Hushed Prayers

In secret places, I whisper low
prayers born of hope, of dreams, of soul-deep glow
on my prayer board, they await Your gentle hand
each one a plea, a longing, a heart's command

Time may stretch, and silence seem to reign
but deep within, I know Your response remains
never a "no", only "yes" or "wait a little while"
patience is refined, trust purified, like silver in fire's trial

My prayer board testifies to Your faithful heart
every request slipped into the "answered" envelope, a
brand new start
proof of Your promises, like sunrise after night
hope renewed, trust restored, in Your loving light

My gratitude jar, once empty, now overflows
with notes of blessing, counted one by one, as day's last
glows
reflecting on Your goodness, my heart swells with praise
thankful for each answer, in Your perfect, timely ways

17. Inked By Your Love

Your ink stains my soul like midnight blue
a permanent mark, a love forever true
on the parchment of my heart, Your words reside
a sacred tattoo, where love and grace abide

With the nib of Your spirit, You inscribe my name
in the ledger of heaven, forever claimed
by the ink of Your blood, my sins erased
a clean page turned, a new story amazed

In the inkwell of Your mercy, my heart dips low
to write the lines of gratitude, forever to grow
with every stroke, my love for You increases
a masterpiece of devotion, in endless releases

Your ink infuses my soul like dye in pure white paper
permanently coloring my heart, a love forever to feature
in the script of Your promises, I find my way
through life's journey, night and day

With each letter, each word, my fate's rewritten
in the ink of eternity, my soul's forever sketched
in divine calligraphy, a love letter to Jesus' heart
sealed with Your signature, my heart's eternal work

18. Above Every Name

My soul is a graveyard of ghosts
where fears and doubts once haunted me
but Jesus brought light to the darkness
and resurrected hope in my heart

His name is above anxiety
it trembles at the sound
of His voice whispering peace
to my frantic mind

His name is higher than depression
it has no grip on my soul
when His love shines brighter
than the darkest nights I've known

His name is stronger than sickness
it heals the deepest wounds
restores the broken pieces
and brings life to my dying bones

His name is louder than heartbreak
it silences the screams
of my shattered heart
and brings solace to my deepest pain

His name is brighter than darkness
it illuminates my path
and guides me through life's storms
to safer shores at last

His name is more powerful than pain
it soothes my deepest hurts
and brings comfort to my soul
like balm to open wounds

His name is my eternal refuge
it shelters me from fear
and wraps me in His loving peace
forever drawing near

19. Love In Every Hue

When blue skies turn to sorrow's grey
and tears fall like autumn rain
know Jesus weeps with you today
His heart empathetic, love unstained

Orange flames of anxiety
may flicker bright with every fear
but His peaceful green pastures await
where love dispels each troubled tear

In yellow bright moments of joy
He celebrates life's simple delight
yet in dark purple nights of pain
His presence remains, a constant light

Dark teal shadows of envy creep
with jealous taunts, "You're not enough"
but Jesus silences them asleep
with truth: His love is your worth

Red emotions raging like a fire
He calms with gentle, loving rain
validating every heart's desire
to be seen, heard, and loved again

His turquoise waters of grace
wash over souls like healing balm
reminding hearts of love's embrace
forever chasing away life's alarm

You are God's canvas, painted with love
You're His masterpiece – He wants you to know from
above.

20. Embers Of Your Name

Your eyes see every hidden thing
my deepest thoughts, darkest everything
yet You listen when I call Your name
voice barely above a whisper, heart in flames

You witness every secret tear
every moment I feel lost, unclear
still Your gentle voice calms my soul
in darkest nights, makes me whole

You hear my every unspoken fear
every anxious thought, every trembling spear
yet Your loving presence draws near
embracing me, dispelling all fear

where You guide, provision follows
like rain soaking dry and barren hollows
reviving hope, restoring life
in Your presence, my heart beats ripe

every step in Your appointed way
resources unfold, come what may
paths uncertain, yet You illuminate
every next step, a gentle create

Your promise stands – "I will provide"
strength for each journey, peace inside
comfort for my soul's deepest night
guiding stars that shine with gentle light

in Your eternal flame, I am refined
purified, transformed – forever
In darkest night
Embers of Your Name, Jesus you always remain

21. My Soul's Eternal Address

Dear Jesus,
lost in darkness, hearts search for the way
You write to us in redemptive ink
"we are loved, regardless of the gray"

Your letter arrives postmarked from above
bearing stamps of sacrifice and endless love
the return address reads "Heaven's Gate"
where Your compassion waits, never late

in Your words, truth resonates deep
"You are the Way, the Life – our soul's escape"
from shadows where we felt too far gone
Your love illuminates the path back home

every line of Your letter whispers low
"we are forgiven, loved, and made anew

Now at last I write a reply letter back to You
Sealed with tears of joy, delivered true
my heart beats only for You
Postmarked to heaven, this letter's sent
forever yours, my soul's consent
Received by Heaven, Accepted by You

www.ingramcontent.com/pod-product-compliance
Lightning Source LLC
LaVergne TN
LVHW051244200726
843510LV00011B/1678